Master the Art of Candle Making

Discover the Joy of Creating Candles with Easy, Step-by-Step Instructions and Vivid Illustrations

By: Evelyn Jacobs

Text Copyright © Lightbulb Publishing

All rights reserved. No part of this guide may be reproduced in any form without permission in writing from the publisher except in the case of brief quotations embodied in critical articles or reviews.

Legal & Disclaimer

The information in this book and its contents are not designed to replace or substitute any form of medical or professional advice. It is not intended to replace the need for independent medical, financial, legal, or other professional advice or services as may be required. The content and information in this book have been provided for educational and entertainment purposes only.

The content and information in this book have been compiled from reliable sources and are accurate to the best of the Author's knowledge, information, and belief. However, the Author cannot guarantee the accuracy and validity and cannot be held liable for errors and/or omissions. Furthermore, changes are made periodically to this book as and when needed.

Where appropriate and/or necessary, you must consult a professional (including but not limited to your doctor, attorney, financial advisor, or such other professional advisor) before using any of the suggested remedies, techniques, or information in this book.

Upon using the contents and information in this book, you agree to hold harmless the Author from and against any damages, costs, and expenses, including any legal fees potentially resulting from the application of any of the information provided. This disclaimer applies to any loss, damages, or injury caused by the use and application, whether directly or indirectly, of any advice or information presented, whether for breach of contract, tort, negligence, personal injury, criminal intent, or under any other cause of action.

You agree to accept all the risks of using the information presented in this book.

You agree by continuing to read this book that, where appropriate and/or necessary, you shall consult a professional (including but not limited to your doctor, attorney, financial advisor, or such other advisor as needed) before using any of the suggested remedies, techniques, or information in this book.

Table of Contents

Chapter 1: Brief History of Candle Making 1
    The Rise of Paraffin, Soy, and Beeswax 3

Chapter 2: Buying and Sourcing Material 7
    Material and Equipment Needed in Candle Making 7
    Core Materials and Tools 7
    Secondary Materials and Tools 20
    Five Sources to Shop Candle Material 24
    Frequently Asked Questions 28

Chapter 3: Mastering the Art from Melting to Pouring 31
    Step by Step guide to making Container Candles 32
    Step-by-Step Guide to Making Mold Candles 41

Chapter 4: Comprehensive Solutions to Candle Issues 51
    Guide to Common Issues 52

Chapter 5: Basic Candle Burn Test 75
    Burn Test Checklist 75

Chapter 6: Decorate and Customize Your Candles 79
    Molds Candles 79
    Container Candles 81

Chapter 7: Best Scent Combinations for Candles 85
    Best Fragrance Combinations - Year Round 88

Chapter 8: Starting A Homemade Candle Business 91
    Step by Step guide to Starting your Candle Business 92
    Ways to Stand Out in Your Business 98

Glossary 101

Chapter 1

Brief History of Candle Making

The word candle finds its origin in the Latin word "candela," which means "to shine." With a rich history of 5000 years, the candles were used to illuminate space, aid travelers, signal during wars, and commence religious rituals. In 164 BC, the Jews used to burn candles in their festival of Lights called "Hanukkah," and The Greeks paid homage to their goddess Artemis. References to candles are given in the Bible, and Emperor Constantine is documented to have used candles during Easter service in the 4th century.

Dated back to ancient civilizations, the Egyptians set the precedent for candle-making by soaking the reed in melted wax without the use of wicks. It was not until 3000 BC that Egyptians shifted to wicked candles, and right after that, ancient Romans employed an innovative technique of dipping rolled papyrus in melted tallow. The Japanese wax was extracted from tree nuts, and Indians contributed by boiling cinnamon trees. Soon, tallow candles were substituted with beeswax and the first scented candle sprang up. The invention of beeswax was a noteworthy advancement, offering an eco-friendly cleaner burn without producing smoky flames. However, the exclusivity of beeswax, owing to its high price, reserved its use for religious rituals only.

The discovery of spermaceti wax, acquired through crystallizing sperm whale oil, marked a turning point during the Middle Ages, owing to its durability, hardness, and brightness, compared to tallow and beeswax versions. These candles were best fit for decorative purposes, setting themselves apart from conventional use. Historians mentioned that the first "standard candles" were made from spermaceti wax, signifying a remarkable stride in candle history. The 15th century marked itself popular for the Chandler candles, an era characterized by full-fledged experiments. The candle makers experimented with different waxes and explored better techniques, including molding and dipping. In the colonial era across America, women emerged as innovators who led the discovery of a new wax by boiling bayberries. This wax was not only functional but infused a delightful aroma with its sweet smell.

In the 19th century, chemists made breakthroughs that paved the way for the development of stearic wax and stearic candles. Joseph Morgan invented machines to produce Molds, breaking barriers to conventional hand practices. The addition of new technologies, such as steam engines, was a step forward to mass production to meet the increasing demand of customers. The candles became available in different shapes, sizes, and colors, which escalated the interest of customers, and soon, in the 1990s, a huge surge in the popularity of scented candles was observed.

The craft of candle making evolved with the use of modern technologies, novel materials, and innovative techniques, and the candles have come a long way. Today, candles are no longer used as a major source of light but as an integral part of home decor, defining versatility, comfort, and elegance. The advent of different types of waxes, fragrance oils, and Molds opened a plethora of boundaries in candle making art.

The Rise of Paraffin, Soy, and Beeswax

- **Beeswax**

    Beeswax was the first wax used in the Middle Ages. This wax is natural and produced from honeybees, which makes it an eco-friendly option for candle making. Not only this, but beeswax candles are also hypoallergenic and discharge a stream of negative ions when burned, which may facilitate purifying the air. Beeswax candles have a long burning span and produce less to no toxins. Emitting a subtle odor of honey, the wax is further complimented with fragrance oils to enhance the scent. Beeswax can be used in a variety of colors and shapes ranging from taper, pillar, and votive., making them a popular choice for both home decor and aromatherapy.

    beeswax: Naturally yellowish in colour.

- **Paraffin Wax**

Paraffin wax, a by-product of petroleum jelly, has gained a foothold in the market for its affordability, availability, better texture, and offering the best hot throw any other wax. The popularity and emergence of paraffin wax, coupled with molds, offered an aesthetic value to the customers, as well as accent home decor. The only drawback of paraffin is the low melting point, which can be overcome by the addition of stearic acid. Since paraffin wax is the most economical, it is produced in large quantities and sold to wholesalers to operate their small and large businesses.

- **Soy Wax**

The environmental concerns and emission of harmful toxins intrigued the chemist to develop a wax composed of sustainable materials, and that's exactly how soy wax came into being. Soy wax derived from soybeans proved to be an exemplary shift towards renewable options. The advantages, however, extend beyond eco-friendly nature. The lower melting point of soy wax extends its longevity, giving it a cleaner burn than paraffin wax. The diversity of soy wax is huge and can be used for a variety of types, including container candles, pillar candles, and tea lights, available in a diverse range of scents and colors. Overall, soy candles stand out as a mindful and versatile alternative with ecological responsibility for a sustainable environment.

Characteristics	Beeswax	Soy Wax	Paraffin Wax
Emissions	No toxins. Emits a sweet scent of honey	No to minimal toxins	High toxins and black flame
Typical Burn time	29 hours	18 hours	15 hours
Cost	Expensive	Moderate	Cheap
Fragrance Load capacity	6-10%	5-12%	4-6%
Hot throw (HT)	Moderate	Good	Strong
Cold throw (CT)	Light	Moderate	Good
Color	Golden-yellow	Beige and creamy	Transparent
Melting point	144-147 F	120-180 F	99-150 F

Chapter 2

Buying and Sourcing Material

Material and Equipment Needed in Candle Making

Many candle makers struggle with acquiring the right materials because there are always ample products to procure. While purchasing the entire range seems overwhelming, it is wiser to begin with essentials to get started. Once you master the skill of candle making, you can always upgrade and switch to better ones to sustain quality and offer top-notch products. Choosing the right supplies allows you to learn the intricate details of crafting candles. This chapter serves as a comprehensive guide to choosing and sourcing basic to advanced candle making material that you need to make premium quality candles. This equipment does not commit to making every category of candle since there are tons to learn, but it will ensure that you have the basic candle guide.

Core Materials and Tools

Candle Wax

Candle wax serves as one of the two indispensable products in candle making. There is a multitude of waxes that you can explore and experiment with to finalize the best fit for you. Each variety of wax has a distinct set of characteristics in different temperature ranges, and therefore, test and trial is the key to unlocking the creative realm. Plain wax is a beginner-free, inexpensive version of wax that is free from additives. This versatile wax can be used to craft an array of candles such as containers, pillars, tea lights, etc, adding a touch of aesthetic to your space. The most readily available and widely embraced wax is soy wax and paraffin wax. They both have their unique traits, and these two waxes can be blended in different ratios for better outcomes. The other waxes are beeswax, coconut wax, gel wax, and palm wax, each holding pros and cons.

Dos

- Test varied waxes at different room temperatures.

- Examine your purpose. If you long for environmentally friendly wax, paraffin wax is an absolute no. You may choose either soy wax or beeswax.

- If you are making scented candles, be aware that every individual wax has disparate fragrance-holding capacity.

- Explore how wax can be blended for pinnacle results. Soy paraffin blend is the most prevailing for pillar candles.

- Remember: TESTING IS THE KEY!

Donts

- Refrain from selecting wax based only on price range. Paraffin wax costs the least but has ecological effects and subpar finishing.

- Do not presume that all-natural wax performs in the same way. Container and pillar candles demand distinct waxes. Pillar candles require sturdy wax to withstand its shape.

Containers

Selecting an appropriate container is not just essential for holding wax but for elevating your candle design as well. From minimal glass jars to wooden bowls, the possibilities are endless. Some materials perform better than others, and only the adequate concordance of container, wick, and wax can yield a top-notch candle for you. Some ubiquitous heat-resistant vessels are mason jars, frosted jars, glass jars, and metal and aluminium tins. Ceramic and wood bowls are oftentimes repurposed to propose an old-world charm and an earthy touch to your candles.

Dos

- Examine your wax before choosing your jar. Several waxes do not adhere effectively, and the finishing falls short.

- Retain the size of the room within your mind. The smaller containers are not designed for larger rooms, as the fragrance does not disperse properly.

- Remember: TESTING IS THE KEY!

Donts

- In no manner should you use jars and vessels that are crafted with flammable materials. Rule out plastic jars.

Candle Wick

Candlewick is as requisite as candle wax, given that candles are incapable of burning without them. The foremost concern, however, is that your candle is burning at an optimal rate. If your wick is too large for the container, your candle will melt fast, even if you have used the best-quality wax. On the contrary, if your wick is too thin for the container, your wick will burn gradually. This culminates in tunneling, and the fragrance will not disperse properly in your space. Therefore, choosing the right size for your wick cracks most candle-related issues.

The size of the wick hinges on the diameter of the container. CD, ECO, wooden, HP, LX, and HTP wicks hold the upper hand in the market. Amidst every type, there is an extensive diversity of sizes. Producers and distributors affix a label with a number at each wick. These wicks are attached with wick stickers. Many makers also make use of hot glue or resistant glue to stick the wick into the container. Although candle wick offers a broad spectrum of materials, the most common, frequently used, and readily available wicks are

Wick type	Composition	Wax type
Cotton wick	Braided cotton fibres	Suitable for soy, paraffin, beeswax, and more
Wooden wick	Thin flat wood	Best for soy and coconut wax
Wax coated wick	Cotton wick coated in wax	Most of the candle waxes

Dos

- Assess your wax type and container size to select your wick accordingly.

- Check the burn pool. The wax is meant to reach up to the edges of the container. The ideal wick should not induce tunneling and extend to a complete melt pool (¼" for each inch of the container in one hour). To give an example if your container is 3", it should attain a complete melt pool in 3 hours.

- Try different wick materials and sizes to know what suits you.

- Remember: TESTING IS THE KEY!!!!

Donts

- Do not overlook your container size.

- Do not ignore the flame size. An ideal wick flame should be between ½" to 1". If your wick flame is too large, it's because you are making use of the wrong wick. Also, some waxes inherently produce a larger flame. Not to mention, paraffin wax has a larger flame than soy wax.

Buying and Sourcing Material

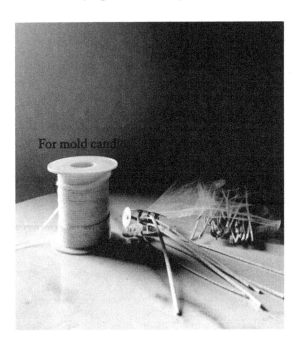

Measuring Scale

If you do not want your wax to go to waste or grapple with preparing the wax on a loop, you must have a measuring scale for calculating wax and fragrance oils. Crafting a well-scented candle demands accurate measurements, and therefore, you need to invest in the right things to achieve consistent results. Consistency is imperative to build trust and credibility, saving cost and time in the long run.

Dos

- Invest in a digital scale that offers quick measurements at the highest level of precision and accuracy.
- Procure a scale that is constricted with durable material, considering it a prolonged investment.

Donts

- Avoid scales that show fluctuating or inconsistent readings.

- Do not invest in a scale that can show readings up to a limited weight.

Pouring Pot

Pouring pot performs multi-faceted tasks. It not only melts your wax but also acts as a support to pour into your required container and vessel. The pouring pot is typically composed of heavy-duty aluminium and steel which are good conductors of heat, followed by hassle-free cleaning.

Dos

- Invest in good material. Stainless Steel pots outshine the glass ones. A lot of wax goes to waste in glass pots because glass has better adherence than steel.

- Always know your batch size prior to buying a pouring pot. Investing in one large pot rather than buying a few small pots is better and more effective.

Donts

- Refrain from buying pots with poor spout design and uncomfortable handles. The pot should ensure clean and mess-free pouring.

- Avoid plastic pots, even if they are of the most premium quality.

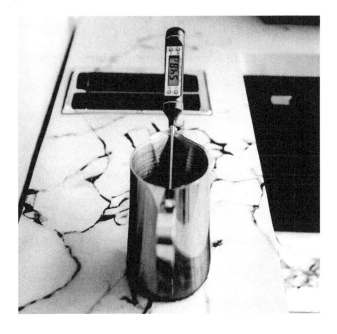

Wick Holders

A Wick holder is a crucial tool for both container and pillar candles, serving the core objective of keeping the wick cantered. Many people pay no attention to it and end up having non-centred wick. When you are pouring the wax, your wick loses sturdiness and sway along the sides. If not used, this leads to grave troubleshooting, such as uneven burning, tunnelling, or extinguishing as the wax is melted on either side of the jar. You will need to use a wick holder until it solidifies to attain a complete burn pool and optimal fragrance release. Oftentimes, metal wick holders are used but modern wick holders are made up of wooden and plastic material as well.

Dos

- Invest in the right heat-resistant material that is durable and sturdy enough to withstand extreme temperatures.

Donts

- Do not use a wick holder that is not compatible with your wick size to promote a balanced burn.

Fragrance and Essential Oils

If you are planning to make scented candles, essential and fragrance oils are core products. The fragrance oils offer better hot and cold throw than essential oils as essential oils are more volatile in nature. The essential oils offer a subtle scent, while the fragrance oils deliver long-lasting and stronger scents. On the flip side, the essentials are also used for therapeutic properties that make them expensive. One example is lavender oil, best known for calming properties and promoting better sleep, while tea tree oils are used for boosting immunity.

Dos

- Invest in good quality oils that can contribute to overall supreme quality, let alone hot throw only. High-quality fragrance oils tend to have better longevity and strength.

- Consider the therapeutic properties of those oils and align them with your purpose.

- Remember: TESTING IS THE KEY!

Donts

- More fragrance oil never means better hot and cold throw. You need to search the typical fragrance-holding capacity of waxes and then experiment with ratios. It is best recommended to use optimal range. Soy wax works well at 8% fragrance oil.

- Always check the safety label on fragrance oils. Some oils can also cause potential health risks and pose allergic reactions.

Thermometer

A thermometer might not look like a necessity, but it is undoubtedly essential to monitor the temperature of scented candles. The fragrance must bind strongly with the wax, and that requires melting wax until a specific temperature is reached. Typically, soy wax needs to be heated until 170-185 F for the best hot throw. The thermometer also guarantees that your wax is not overheated as such, wax encounters discoloration and degradation. While pouring, you need to cool down your wax as temperature fluctuations may cause sinkholes and cracking in the wax.

Dos

- Invest in a high-quality digital thermometer that gives accurate readings and is easier to read than manual ones.

- Clean your thermometer with a tissue before every use for precise reading.

Donts

- Handle the thermometer delicately and refrain from storing it in place at extreme temperatures. This can lead to reduced precision and inaccurate readings.

- Never leave your thermometer in the wax for too long, as prolonged heat can cause significant damage.

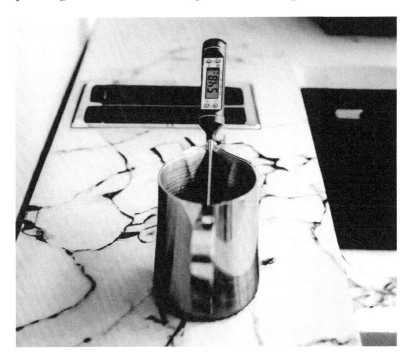

Heat Gun

The purpose of the heat gun is to remelt the wax and allow it to solidify again in the container for seamless tops and neat finishing. A multitude of makers have put hairdryers to use as an alternative to heat guns. This can be a potential choice if you do not want to invest much, but hairdryers are not devised for higher temperatures and swift results. Additionally, a heat gun is designed to heat the containers prior to pouring to avoid temperature fluctuations that can lead to cracking or other troubleshooting. Simply put, this tool is used to heat containers, address uneven surfaces, repair frosting, and ensure smooth finishing.

Dos

- Shop the heat gun with diverse temperature, power, and speed settings so you can control it as per your requirements.

Donts

- Do not pass over safety concerns. Ensure that your heat gun has safety mechanisms, such as a cool-down function and a stable base, to prevent accidents.

Secondary Materials and Tools

Molds

With evolution, the candle makers advanced in introducing innovative candles and shifted from container to pillar candles. This demanded molds that are used to shape liquid wax into diverse shapes and sizes. Today, pillar and motive candles are the most sought-after products, presenting a unique approach to expressing your artistic preferences. Metal, plastic, and silicone are the three types of materials offered in molds. Plastic molds are highly priced, followed by silicon and steel molds, owing to cost factors. It is because plastic and silicone molds have an upper hand in finishing. The candle makers make candles for animals, festivals, letters, and much more that are sold in markets at expensive prices.

Dos

- Do not neglect the description of dimensions before buying molds, particularly while purchasing the products online.

- Explore different shapes and varieties to add creativity and elegance to your space.

Donts

- Do not compromise on quality and shop. Do not use cheap molds, as they give poor finishing and pose difficulties while wicking.

- Do not overlook the compatibility of your wax and molds. For example, paraffin wax has high adhering properties, and silicon mold is best for this type of wax.

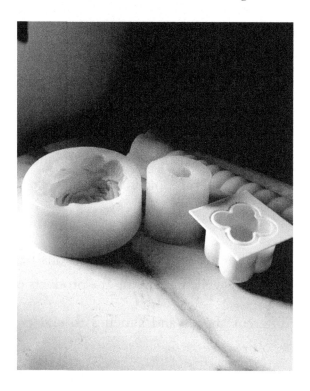

Wick Needle, Wick Trimmer, and Wick Snuffer

This trio is a combination of not-necessary but supplementary tools to facilitate your candlemaking process. Wicking a thick mold is no less than a nightmare, and a wick needle, also known as a "wick pin," is a metal or stainless steel slender tool used to thread the mold easily. Wick trimmers are scissor-like trimmers comprised of long shears and circular blades that are used to trim the additional wick, either in container or pillar candles. Wick care is mandatory, and therefore, these trimmers are used to cut ½ inch of wick after every use to prevent excessive flame. After you are done burning the candle, the wick snuffer is used to extinguish the candle without blowing it to avoid smoke.

Dos

- These prolonged tools should be crafted with corrosion-resistant and high-quality material.

Donts

- Do not ignore the sizes of products such that your wick needle has a thicker hole than your wick and the wick snuffer is large enough to not let any smoke escape in the surrounding.

Candle Dyes

Adding dye to your candles has been imperative to enhance the visual appearance of candles. These candle dyes are in the form of liquid or chips that are blended well with colorless wax to infuse a vibrant look. From neutral tones to colorful hues, these dyes are great sources to align with events, festivals, and fluctuating seasons and tailor it as per customer preferences.

Dos

- Choose the concentrated dye that formulates well with your wax. For instance, liquid dyes are considered to be best as these dyes seamlessly blend with all types of waxes but high-quality powder and chip dyes are no less.

- Remember: TESTING IS THE KEY!

Donts

- Do not neglect environmental impact and prioritize sustainability, as several dyes are composed of toxic materials.

- Do not choose dyes based solely on price. Some dyes are inexpensive but offer muted colors and have great environmental impacts.

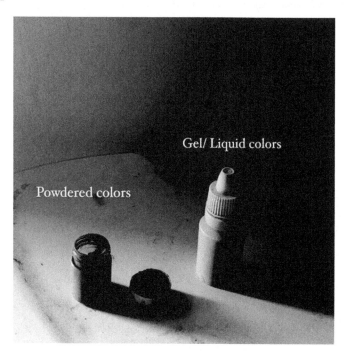

Five Sources to Shop Candle Material

Local vendors

The local vendors are invaluable resources for procuring material in the most effortless and hassle-free way. Establishing a good relationship with local vendors enables you to bargain and acquire the goods at the cut-rate price. Fostering effective communication means you can get personalized items that might not be possible with online shopping. On-site shopping also allocates choice to shop from a wide array of materials ranging from waxes to dyes. Not to mention, sourcing material from local vendors will reduce delivery charges for each product, ensuring timely delivery as fast as possible.

Pros

- Cost-effective
- Quality assurance
- Personalized products

Cons

- Limited material

Amazon

Amazon is an e-commerce one-stop platform that stands as a substantial market for a comprehensive range of home decor and small business supplies, including candlemaking materials. The colossal volume of local to high-end products allows customers to shop extensive products at different price ranges without commuting. From different candle waxes to high-quality fragrance oils, you will find everything under one platform. Note that before buying, it is imperative to take customer's reviews and ratings into your consideration to avoid bad experiences.

Pros

- Convenience
- Variety
- Customer reviews

Cons

- Shipping costs
- Shipping delays
- Quality control

Ali Express

Ali Express is an international online retail platform based in China that connects sellers and buyers across the globe to shop for a variety of products. Due to its competitive pricing, this is an attractive option for small-business owners. One can find tons of candlemaking supplies, from individual products to basic candlemaking kits, on this platform. Before buying the products, it is pivotal to engage with the sellers and communicate your concerns to avoid misunderstandings.

Pros

- Cost-effective
- Global reach
- Deals and discounts

Cons

- Shipping time
- Communication barrier

Etsy

Etsy is best known for its innovation in handmade items ranging from clothing to home decor. All the information is enlisted under products that allow users hassle-free shopping in the heaven of hand-crafted items made with love. Due to its emphasis on modern and unique art, Etsy supports small-business owners but also ensures transparency through seller feedback and product reviews to facilitate buyers.

Pros

- Creative items
- Small businesses ideal
- Customization

Cons

- Limited products
- Shipping cost
- High prices

Candle Science

A wide-reaching audience uses candle science products because of its credibility of delivering high-quality and beginner-friendly products in no time. Candle Science is purely dedicated to candle makers, who not only shop for candle supplies but also read informative blogs to make better-scented candles. With its extensive research on making scented candles, with supplies guides via tutorials and blogs on different wax types, wick sizes, and more, it is an invaluable asset that no other channel does better than candle science.

Pros

- Quality assurance

- Diverse range

Cons

- High-priced

- Shipping cost

Frequently Asked Questions

Why does my candle wax take time to heat?

Some waxes are studier than others. Soy wax and coconut wax are soft and, therefore, have lower melting points than paraffin wax. This allows the wax to melt more rapidly than other waxes, and it has nothing to do with the quality of the wax. Also, the heat source and heat intensity may additionally influence the heating process.

Which wick should I choose for my candle?

The ideal wick size should be compatible with the container and wax. The vessels with larger diameters will need a thicker wax than smaller diameters jars to attain a full melt pool. To choose that, one needs to do testing. The type of candle also influences the wick type. For instance, Pure cotton wicks are better for container candles, while braided wicks are suitable for pillar candles. An ideal wick should pass through a full melt pool, with less soot and flame production and optimal fragrance release.

Can I mix different fragrance oils?

The fragrance oils can be blended to offer better hot and cold throws. However, it is important to keep ratios in mind for personal customization. It is better to test on small batches first and check if the fragrances are diluted properly.

How do I clean my molds?

It is best to remove leftover wax followed by rinsing it in warm water and cleaning it with soapy water afterward using a tissue or soft brush. Make sure that you do not clean aggressively to avoid cracks and stretch lines on molds.

How to stick the wick to my containers?

While wicks can be directly stuck with hot wax and even several additives like hot glue, it is best to make use of Wick stickers. These wick stickers allow a hassle-free and convenient method of sticking the wicks to the containers.

Can I reuse my leftover wax?

Unscented wax can be used together. For scented wax, make sure that both waxes have the similar scent.

Chapter 3

Mastering the Art from Melting to Pouring

There are a gazillion reasons why candles have gained a foothold in the international markets lately. They are complete mood-setters, offering serenity and coziness. The hobby of candlemaking seems entertaining and effortless until you discover that your candles smell poorly. This might get on your nerves, holding you into a cluster of questions like ifs, whys, and buts. Whether you are a beginner, diving into this fun hobby, or a skilled candle-maker down to sell your products, this chapter serves as a gateway to the beyond-conventional candlemaking process for both container and mold candles, depicting how these two processes interlink but also differ from each other. Through this guide, you will realize that this alchemy is not a one-size-fits-all thing but incorporates subtle nuances of tests and creativity between wax, wicks, scents, colors, and pour methods that transform your boring candle into an aesthetically pleasing handmade product.

Here are seven steps to make the best-scented candles in containers

Step by Step guide to making Container Candles

Prepare the Workspace

A well-maintained workspace means a systematic workflow, leading to a hurdle-free candlemaking process. This does not necessarily mean that you need an enormous or stunning workspace but rather a comfortable studio where you can undertake your tasks to generate exemplary quality candles. Before everything else, declutter all the redundant items and spruce up your space to prevent accumulated dust and debris. Under your one workspace, ensure that you delegate each area for an individual purpose. This means you will have segregated sections for storing equipment, pouring, and, eventually, an area for packaging. Some materials, such as fragrance oils and wax, must be safeguarded against sun exposure as they can hold the potential to deteriorate the quality of products. Finally, here is the checklist of all the products that you will need to make container candles

- Wax
- Wicks
- Container
- Thermometer
- Wick stickers
- Fragrance oils
- Spatula
- Double boiler
- Candle colors (if any)
- Measuring scale
- Pouring pot

Choose, Measure, and Melt the Wax

One core essential in making candles, either scented or unscented, is wax. Therefore, the process starts with choosing an appropriate wax and measuring it to meet your specifications.

- People choose the wax that best fits their purpose. According to research, the most prevalent and widely used is soy wax, owing to its ability to deliver eco-friendly and cleaner burns.

- Choose a wax that does not shrink much, as shrinkage may contribute to uneven burn, generating large sinkholes at the center and inciting other challenges. Generally, paraffin wax is deemed to have more shrinkage than other waxes.

- For measuring wax, opt for a measuring scale that delivers accurate results. If you do not have a measuring scale, the rough estimate is that two pounds of wax will fill approximately five 8-oz Mason jars (jam jars or half-pints) or 10 4-oz jelly jars.

- A large influx of beginners directly melt the wax in the oven, which is the most unfavorable and dangerous way. Always go for the double-boiler method. This means that you need to heat the water in one boiler, pour the wax into the pouring pot, and place the pouring pot in the boiler. This process must be done in medium heat settings.

- This is followed by constant stirring using a spatula to maintain a steady temperature and avoid the formation of wax lumps. Each wax has its melting points, so do not worry if one wax melts faster than the other.

- Also, remember that you do not have to wax melt until it transforms to a liquid state but until it is pure from all the contaminants and able to bond well with fragrance oil.

- While choosing an appropriate wax, it is important to consider its source, appearance, burn, fragrance-holding capacity, and environmental impacts. Our top picks for container candles are

    - Soy: Golden Brands 464 Soy Wax

    - Paraffin: IGI 4627 Comfort Blend Wax

    - Blend: IGI 6006 Soy/Paraffin Blend Wax

Check Temperature

While making scented candles that last long and deliver a strong scent, DO NOT NEGLECT THE TEMPERATURE. Making well-scented candles is all about maintaining temperature and fragrance.

- Use a digital thermometer to yield precise readings.

- An optimal temperature of 170-185 F is well-suited to most waxes, especially natural soy wax. However, make sure that you check the correct specifications for your wax grade.

Add Fragrance Oil and Colour

Fragrance oil is not to be introduced without weighting. It's because mastering the art of adding appropriate fragrance oil to your wax will craft top-notch candles.

- Choose the type of fragrance you want to work with to kick things off. This includes floral, fruity, earthy, woody, spicy, warm, sweet, citrus, herbal, aquatic, and seasonal scents.

- Fragrance and essential oils are very expensive, so instead of experimenting, choose the best-selling or popular fragrance oils. We recommend buying from candle science since they have a huge variety of premium-quality fragrance oils. You can also shop from local vendors and online platforms at cheap prices if you do not want to invest much into high-quality fragrance oil and candlemaking, which is more like a hobby than a business.

- Every wax has a different fragrance-holding capacity, so double-check the percentage for your wax.

- Soy wax has a 6-12% fragrance holding capacity and in case you want to skip testing, which you should not, we recommend using 8% FO. This means if your container has 100 g of wax, you will add 10 g of fragrance oil to it. If you do not have a measuring cup, this makes 15-20 drops in 1 gram of oil.

- After removing the pouring pot from the stove, start adding fragrance at the required temperature (185 F for soy wax), and make sure that you stir it slowly for at least two minutes so that your wax and fragrance oil bond together to give off a powerful scent when burnt.

Prepare the Container

- Before pouring, you need to gear up for pre-preparing your containers. This step simplifies a lot of things.

- Select a container that complements your interest, but check up on heat-resistant materials such as tins, ceramics, and glass. Glass containers, although they look aesthetically pleasing as they are transparent, can potentially crack during extreme temperatures.

- If you do not have any containers at the moment, you can always repurpose previous glass and mason jars.

- Ensure that you clean your containers with a cloth to remove any dust and debris.

- Choose a suitable wick material and size according to the diameter of your vessel. The most commonly used wicks are cotton wicks, given that they have a cleaner burn. According to candle science, these are the wicks that are well-suited for the following waxes.

Wicks	Wax
CD Wick Series	Soy Wax Paraffin IGI 6046(Coconut Paraffin blend)
ECO Wick Series	Soy Wax Paraffin IGI 6006 (Para Soy blend)
LX Wick Series	Soy Wax (Eco Soya CB-135, CB-Advanced and Pillar Blend (PB) Paraffin: IGI 4625 and 4630

Pour wax

Excelling in the art of pouring wax into the vessel requires practice and rigorous strategies to achieve visually pleasing outcomes. Skilled candle makers might know the importance of pouring methods, but beginners often neglect them, ending up with tons of challenges.

- The ideal method is to initially allow the wax to cool around 125-135 F and then pour it slowly into the container to facilitate smooth and even distribution without causing adhesion and shrinkage issues. Fast pouring means inviting air bubbles in your candles, which can cause large sinkholes.

- Many candle-makers swear by the double pour method, which involves pouring the wax into layers. This method might be time-consuming, but it also affirms that your candle is protected from the risk of sinkholes, uneven surfaces, and air bubbles.

- Following the pouring of wax, make use of a wick holder to center the wick and foster a uniform appearance.

- Abstain from placing lids over your jars until the candle has properly cooled. This might take up to three hours. Placing the lid on your jar will cause fluctuations in temperature and may potentially cause condensation on the lid of the container.

- After your candle has cooled, make sure to check if it has a smooth surface with no sinkholes. If not, do invest in a good heat gun. Set the heat gun to low-to-medium heat settings and remelt the wax. Never put it to high settings, as it can cause the wax to splash at the edges of the container. Maintain a safe distance with the heat gun and do not overheat the wax or else it will lose its structure and characteristics.

- Allow it to cool again. This time, you will have a smooth surface.

Trim wick

- Trim the excessive wick with a wick trimmer or a nail cutter. Refrain from using scissors as they can flatten or crush the wick, which can negatively impact the performance of the candle.

- Cut the wick around ¼ above the candle's surface and make sure to cut it after each burn to sustain its life.

- Enjoy your scented candle with the best hot and cold throw.

Step-by-Step Guide to Making Mold Candles

Select the Mold

The market is full of beautiful molds for every occasion, and selecting the right mold that can produce the finest quality is crucial. Molds come in three major materials: Silicon, metal, and plastic.

- Silicon molds are most widely used because of their top-notch finishing, adhering properties, intricate designs, and easy unmolding without damaging the piece. This mold is more durable than other versions, but while selecting the silicon mold, it is imperative to invest in a high-quality mold that can be sustained and last for years.

- While waxes can change the outcome, silicon molds work well for most waxes, such as paraffin, soy, and beeswax.

- Do not forget to read the description of the inner and outer dimensions of the mold to accurately produce all small and large-sized candles.

- One final thing is to make sure that your mold is heat-resistant and can withstand the hot temperature of liquid wax without warping and deforming to maintain a consistent candle shape.

Prepare the Mold

Preparing the mold before pouring wax not only saves time but effort, too.

- To prepare the mold, clean it thoroughly with a tissue or thin cloth. Make sure you do not clean it rigorously, as it will introduce scratches and degrade the quality of the candles.

- After cleaning, it's the right time to go ahead with wicking. A large spool of cotton wick is suitable for the mold candles.

- While choosing the right wick, do not forget the diameter of the mold and wax type. A lot of candle makers prime the wick in the wax not only to enhance and prolong burning but to intensify the fragrance release as well.

- Now, wick the mold with the help of a needle. While wicking, make sure you are not using a very thick needle that can puncture the mold; instead, a thin and sharp needle can penetrate and fulfill its function.

- After wicking, it's time to center the mold with the help of a wick holder. For relatively larger molds, one wick causes tunneling, so two or more wicks are used for even distribution.

- Some candle makers use a thick wick that can cause a large melt pool and disperse the fragrance in less to no time. While this technique might be promising to scatter the fragrance, it will eventually reduce the burn time and melt within a few minutes.

Opting for a wick that burns longer and releases a subtle fragrance holds the solution.

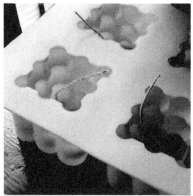

Wicking Mold   Preparing Molds

Selecting and Melting wax

Selecting a wax for mold candles is different than container candles.

In container candles, you pay no heed to the sturdiness of wax while in mold candles, it is crucial so that your candles can withstand their weight. While the main concern with container wax is its adhesion and shrinkage, the wax for mold candles should be hard and durable.

Our top picks of wax for mold candles are

- Beeswax: Ideal for pillar candles and has a high melting point

- Stearic wax: It is like beeswax, offering cleaner and even burn

- Soy wax: Soy pillar wax for cleaner burn. Best for environmentally conscious consumers

- Paraffin wax or Soy Paraffin blend: It is versatile and affordable but emits black smoke.

To enhance the hot throw and make candles burn longer by making them sturdy, some additives like stearic acid with a typical percentage of 3% to 10% and vybar with a typical percentage of 0.5% to 2% are introduced and melted with the wax. Small batch tests are conducted to know the exact percentage and formulation that works best for your wax and wicks

- To melt the wax, use a double boiler method at medium flame. Monitor the wax and melt it around 170-185 F to remove contaminants.

Adding Fragrance and Colours

Infusing vibrant colors and aromatic fragrances in mold candles requires innovative techniques coupled with creativity and precision. Each color and each fragrance hold a different power, and therefore, we need to test, test, and test.

- Blending fragrances necessitates carefully testing each fragrance in different ratios. It's advisable to follow recommended fragrance load guidelines, which may vary based on the wax type, to avoid issues like poor burn performance or fragrance oil seepage.

- Introducing colors in pillar and mold candles opens a scads of possibilities in the creative realm. The colors come in liquid dyes, color blocks, and powder form.

- The tip here is to start with a conservative amount and check the color constantly changing from lighter shades to darker shades. For color blocks, cut them into fine blocks so that the color is dispersed evenly in the wax. Remember: A little color goes a long way, and an excessive number of colors can impact the quality.

- According to many skilled candle-makers, liquid dyes mix well and offer consistent color, while powder ones generally settle at the bottom.

- Avoid the use of mica powder. Although it has a fine texture, it can form clumps and generally migrate or bleed the color toward the burning area.

Pour the Wax

In the final stage of mold candle making, the pouring process demands attention to detail, complemented by modern insights and time-tested techniques.

- Before pouring, make sure to preheat the molds with the help of a heat gun. This reduces temperature variations and frosting, allowing the wax to cool at a steady rate. Preheating the mold also helps in better adhesion.

- Now pour the wax very slowly and from the ends of the mold. Through slow pouring, you reduce the risk of air bubbles. This is followed by gently tapping each side of the mold. A vibration table can also be used to dislodge any entrapped bubbles.

- Allow it to cool for a few hours.

Unmold

- Before unmolding, be certain that your wax has properly solidified, or else you will break your beautiful, detailed candle into pieces.

- For smooth extraction, put your mold in the freezer for at least 5 minutes to ensure proper adhesion and avoid breakage.

- Gently remove from the edges and corners of the mold. Keep rotating, and after it has been removed from every edge, go deep, hold the wick, and push it from the centre. Avoid pulling it too hard or too fast to prevent distortion.

Trim and enjoy

- Now, the final step is to trim, burn, and enjoy the aroma of a scented candle.

- Make sure to trim and leave ¼ inch to ½ inch above the surface.

- Before burning, it is advisable to cure the candle for a few days (typically one week) as it enhances the fragrance and quality.

- Burn it after a few days and enjoy the intricate details infused with a strong aroma.

Chapter 4

Comprehensive Solutions to Candle Issues

Candle fanatics pour heart and soul into crafting visually appealing and aesthetic candles, yet they encounter myriad challenges in the middle of the candlemaking process. The greatest share of problems stem from choosing inappropriate wick size, whereas the rest are linked to wax, temperature fluctuations, and more. Therefore, from wax to wick, candle makers need to pay attention to understanding material performance under different conditions. This chapter is a troubleshooting guide for a wide spectrum of minor and major candle issues to master the perfection of candle art.

Here is a list of the most common troubles covered in this chapter.

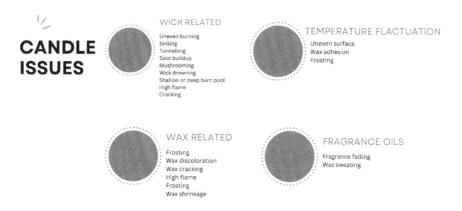

Guide to Common Issues

Uneven Burning

What is Uneven Burning?

Uneven burning is the condition where the wax melts at one side of the container, leaving some areas with excess wax while some parts are not burnt evenly. It is largely caused when the wick is not positioned properly. Therefore, the candle makers take careful consideration and opt for wick holders that may look like an unnecessary item for beginners but hold immense value in the long haul.

What causes Uneven Burning?

Uneven burning is an issue associated with the wrong wick. If you are using a smaller wick or it is not centrally aligned, you may encounter uneven burning. Besides that, different waxes have different melting points, and this property can influence burn rates. Since Paraffin wax is sturdy, it is known for delivering the best burn rate as compared to soy wax and beeswax which are softer.

Therefore, additives such as stearic acid are introduced into these waxes to lengthen the burn rate. Often, the overuse of fragrance oil can potentially cause uneven burning due to the production of excess soot.

How to fix Uneven Burning?

- While preparing candles, make sure to position the wick at the center using a wick holder. The cantered placement is imperative to attain a full melt pool. Through this approach, your candle is protected from tunneling, and the wax extends at the periphery of the container.

- This is not a one-time rule, but you always need to trim your wick to about ½ or ¼ inches after each burn. If not trimmed, your wick will produce a larger flame and burn too hot, which can cause uneven burning.

- If your wick is not aligned, poke holes in the candle and adjust the wick. This must be followed by smoothing the top layer using a heat gun at low to medium settings.

Tunneling

What is Tunnelling?

Tunneling is the condition in which your wick is too short to acquire a full melt pool and, therefore, melts around the center only. This leaves the wax at the edges unburnt and causes a tunnel-like hold at the middle of the candle due to which your wick drowns gradually and burn time is reduced.

What causes Tunnelling?

If your wick is too small for the diameter of your vessel, your wick is not capable of generating enough heat to melt the wax evenly across the edges of the container. If not wick, the wrong composition or using poor quality wax will contribute to tunneling owing to their composition and characteristics. Also, adding too much fragrance oil will alter wax properties once blended. These fragrance oils incorporate high levels of chemicals like vanillin that can accelerate the rate at which the wax solidifies, potentially increasing the likelihood of tunneling.

How to fix Tunnelling?

- Check the diameter of your vessel and pick the wick size appropriately before candle making. A lot of manufacturers offer size guides to buyers, or there are tons of websites that can match your container and wax type with the appropriate wick size. The key is to experiment with different waxes and choose the best fit for your desired container.

- These guides also contain typical fragrance load capacity for different waxes that you need to check to avoid overusing them and falling into the typical range.

- Choosing high-quality and well-formulated waxes can promote even burning and ensure a consistent melt pool.

Soot buildup

What is Soot Buildup?

When there is subpar air circulation, the candle encounters partial combustion. If the wick is too long, the flame does not receive enough oxygen to light and, therefore, produces excess soot. This soot often accumulates at the surface of the container, making the container black. Factors like poorly designed containers or introducing excessively ventilated conditions can restrict airflow and cause inefficient burning.

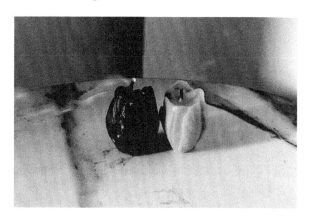

What causes Soot Buildup?

The wrong size of wick plays a pivotal role in soot buildup. If the wick is too large, it will exceed flame output, giving way to soot production. On the contrary, if your wick is below the threshold, it may fall short of burning the wax completely, which contributes to soot buildup. Variations in environmental parameters such as humidity, altitude, or air pollution can affect the performance of candles. Moreover, the built-in properties of certain waxes can also play a part. For instance, Paraffin wax is composed of petroleum products, and it typically discharges black fumes, unlike soy and beeswax. The fragrance oils, additives, and dyes are also contaminated to some extent, and the impurities can potentially increase the likelihood of soot production.

How to Fix Soot Buildup?

Selecting an accurate size of wick holds utmost importance in addressing soot and flame-related concerns. If you are choosing an eco-friendly wick, it will burn cleaner and add to less production of soot despite an average quality wax. Wick testing is preferred in every step of candle making, and candle care is succeeded by candle care, such as cutting the wick before each use to maintain a stable flame.

- Some high-quality waxes, such as soy wax, beeswax, and coconut wax, are more popular on the grounds of their environmental benefits and low soot emotions than traditional waxes.

- An optimal range of fragrances and additives must be included.

- Allow the candle to attain a full melt pool by giving it an appropriate time to burn. Candle extinguishers have been excessively popular in the market to prevent soot emissions in the environment.

Mushrooming

What is Mushrooming?

Mushrooming is one of the most sought-after wick issues in candle making. This refers to the formation of carbon buildup at the tip of the wick, looking like a mushroom. If not addressed, this mushrooming can promote several other challenges, such as the risk of fire, excessive smoke, and reduced hot throw.

What causes Mushrooming?

A large wick that burns fast will soak up more liquid, piling the carbon deposit at the top surface of the wick. Excessive burning turns these deposits into tiny mushrooms. Some waxes, such as Paraffin wax, generate more fumes than soy and beeswax, widely acclaimed for smokeless burns. Flawed formulations of fragrance oils with complex structures can also contribute to pronounced mushrooming.

How to fix Mushrooming?

- Other than typical wick care after each burn, the manufacturers have introduced coated wicks in the market to combat mushrooming. These wicks are covered with special additives such as borax or other waxes that replace mushrooming with low-emission burning.

- While making candles, make sure to opt for pre-waxed wicks for consistent burn.

- High-quality fragrance oils that are well-formulated must be used.

- A four-hour test with three sets is recommended to settle on the perfect wick size.

- Opt for a container that has a wide opening and allows better airflow.

- Avoid over-burning. The candle should not be burnt more than the size of its diameter at one time. For example, If your container has a 3-inch diameter, it should not burn more than three hours each time.

- If mushrooming occurs, trim the carbon buildup and light your candle again.

Wick Drowning

What is Wick Drowning?

Wick drawing is another widely discussed issue that puts both the candle-makers and buyers in trouble as wick cannot be burnt again. It refers to the burial of a wick in melted wax due to excessive oxygen that extinguishes the wick. After the wick is drowned, the candle is of no use.

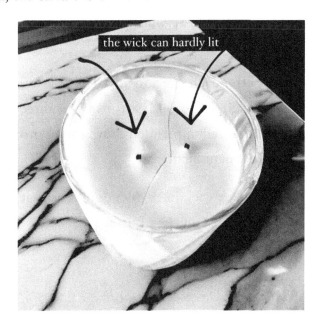

What causes Wick to drown?

If your wick is too small for the container, it may submerge in the surrounding pool of wax. Only a right wick that fits your container size promises consistent burn. Wick drawing stems from several other factors, such as the introduction of highly viscous and dense fragrance oils with additives. Many containers have uneven surfaces and narrow openings that restrict airflow. Due to improper combustion, the wick is drowned.

How to fix Wick Drowning?

- During the candle making process, pay attention to wick size. Do not opt for excessively large wicks, as those can generate a taller flame.

- If the wick is not drowned badly, remove the excess wax from the surrounding area and burn again.

- Trim the wick after each use and adjust the burn time. Do not overburn and maintain to burn it for two or three hours each time. Follow the recommended burn time provided by a reputable candle manufacturer.

- Avoid burning your wick in drafty conditions that can disrupt flame stability or cause uneven burning.

Shallow or Deep Burn Pool

What is a Shallow or Deep burn pool?

Melt pool refers to the amount of surrounding wax in the form of liquid that has spread across the edges of candles. Due to the improper size of the wick and several other factors, your candle encounters too shallow or too deep a burn pool. A shallow melt pool occurs when your wick is too small to burn properly, and a deep pool refers to the condition when your wick is too large to melt the wax swiftly.

Comprehensive Solutions to Candle Issues

Shallow Burn Pool   Deep Burn Pool

What causes Shallow and Deep burn pools?

The shallow burn pool is typically caused by smaller wick and inadequate airflow that causes incomplete combustion, whereas the deep melt pool is caused by larger wick burns for an extended period. Both issues bring numerous other candle-related challenges. While a deep burn pool may seem overwhelming, with fragrance dispersing in the whole area, it can lead to rapid consumption of wax and fire hazards. The container may become excessively hot, and a lot of times, fragile containers such as those made from glass may crack badly. On the flip side, shallow, deep pools cause the wax to melt more rapidly, due to which wick may mushroom, leading to tunneling or sinking. Other potential reasons causing deep or shallow melt pools include wax types, as paraffin wax melts slowly, and therefore, some natural waxes necessitate additives. Fragrance oil, environmental conditions, and improper wick care also culminate in inadequate burn pools.

How to fix a Deep or Shallow burn pool?

- Choosing the right size of the wick is the core solution for smooth and consistent burn. This wick must be selected by considering the diameter size. This means a vessel with a wide opening will require thicker and larger wick than narrow opening containers.

- Additives, dyes, and fragrance oils must be added within their optimal range.

High Flame

What is a High Flame?

High flame refers to the condition when your flame is too high or taller than the desired outcome. High flame can pose dangerous risks, like the candle catching fire or producing excessive heat, so it is crucial to know the causes and control it immediately.

What causes a High Flame?

High flame can be caused by wax and wick. Some waxes, such as paraffin wax, are richer in carbon content than other conventional waxes, so they release more energy. Due to its chemical composition, it gives off a taller flame. Most of the time, the candle makers use larger wicks to deliver better hot throws. Eventually, this causes the wick to burn faster as more wax is consumed and produces a larger flame.

How to Fix a High Flame?

- An adequate blend of proper wax and wick is required to maintain a stable flame. This means using soy or beeswax and opting for the perfect size of wick will deliver the best outcomes, affirming stable flame height.

- A lot of times, burning causes the flame to go taller, so it is recommended to burn for two to three hours per use.

- Candle care that includes trimming the wax is critical to retain.

- Ultimately, your candle must be protected from drafty conditions, and in case of higher flame, do not leave your candle unattended to avoid fire hazards.

Shrinkage and Adhesion Issues

What is the Shrinkage and Adhesion issue?

When your wax does not stick properly to the container and leave room for air bubbles and air pockets, this is referred to as an adhesion problem or an adhesion failure. This is typically caused by shrinkage when the volume of wax is reduced while transitioning from a liquid state to a solid state. However, it does not affect the performance of the candle. It deteriorates the aesthetic of your candle.

What causes Shrinkage and Adhesion issues?

Shrinkage and adhesion issue is primarily caused by temperature fluctuation. When you pour your wax at inappropriate temperatures, either too hot or too cold, your candle does not adhere properly. The uneven cooling pushes the wax to separate from the container, leaving gaps and air pockets and visually affecting the aesthetics of the candle.

How to fix Shrinkage and Adhesion issues?

- Pre-preparation of containers is a paramount step. This means cleaning the interior of the vessel using a tissue or cloth to remove dust, oil moisture, or any debris that can act as a barrier to adhesion.

- Pouring at the right temperature and letting the wax cool gradually is the key. This ensures that there are no entrapped air bubbles or turbulence.

- It is best recommended to avoid transparent containers and instead use amber jars or opaque vessels that can hide adhesion problems.

- Switch to better adhesion waxes, such as Paraffin wax, if environmental concerns are not what you are looking for.

Uneven surface

If the top surface of your candle is not leveled after your wax has solidified completely, it is referred to as an uneven surface. In this case, your surface has irregularities, bumps, and depressions in the form of holes or unlevelled surfaces. Sinking is also a part of an uneven surface when your wax collapses inwards, leading to a huge depression.

What causes Uneven Surfaces?

Between pouring and cooling, there is a persistent shift in temperatures that causes uneven solidification of wax. In this case, some parts of the wax cool more rapidly than others, causing a bumpy surface extending over the entire surface. Improper mixing of additives, fragrance oils, colors, and even inadequate amounts of these essentials can also culminate in uneven texture. Some additives fail to merge properly with the wax and clump together, exacerbating the likelihood of a bumpy surface.

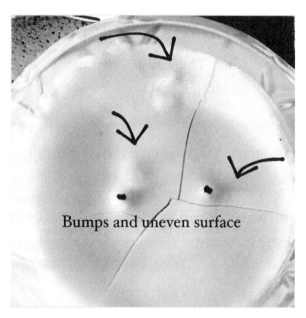

Bumps and uneven surface

How to Fix an Uneven Surface?

Mastering the art of pouring technique can settle uneven surface issues. After your wax has attained its desired temperature, mix everything and blend it well with the wax, followed by constant stirring and waiting.

Preheat the vessels and let the wax cool. Now, pour slowly across the edges. Pouring in a fast motion or from height can introduce air bubbles in the wax.

A heat gun or hairdryer comes to the rescue to combat an uneven surface. Keep your heat gun at low to medium settings and heat your container from a distance. The heat will soften and melt the wax, followed by gradual cooling, which will wipe out all the imperfections.

If you do not have a heat gun, make sure to leave some space during the candlemaking process. If the surface is irregular, remove the remaining wax and add another top layer. This assures an even coverage across the entire surface, offering a smooth covering.

Frosting

Frosting, also referred to as "bloom," is a state where white crystalline patterns are formed at the surface of a candle, giving it a frosted look. This issue is caused by the wax type and has to do with visual aesthetics only. Frosting does not affect the performance of the candle.

What causes Frosting?

Some waxes, such as natural soy wax and beeswax, inherently cause frosting due to their composition. Since these waxes are composed of natural oils and fatty acids, they create frost-like patterns after they are solidified. The frosting is also caused by temperature variation and extreme humidity. If the temperature is too cool and the wax solidifies quickly, it traps air bubbles and moisture within itself, causing a frosted pattern. Also, some additives and fragrance oils having chemicals like vanillin can increase the formation of crystals that enhance the probability of frosting.

How to fix Frosting?

- Selection of the right wax, the right additives, proper pouring techniques, controlling pouring temperature, and minimal exposure to humidity can resolve frosting issues.

- Some additives, such as stearic acid and vybar are used as additives to reduce frosting and enhance the texture of the wax.

- Selection of the right container is equally important as thick-walled opaque containers slow down the cooling process and augment the chances of frosting.

- If you are using wax that has the potential to cause frosting, it is better not to choose transparent or translucent containers. If there is frosting, consider re-pouring a thin layer of wax, but make sure to use the same wax and fragrance oil to maintain consistency.

Fragrance Fading

When the scent of fragrance diminishes over a specific period, the candle does not smell strong, and this phenomenon is called fragrance fading. However, it is obvious that as much as the wax will melt, the fragrance will fade, causing excessive volatility, which demands proper evaluation. This is one of the most asked questions from customers so addressing this issue can help buyers craft long-lasting candles.

What causes fragrance fading?

Poor-quality fragrance oils will make poor candles, just like using top-notch paints is crucial to ending up with the best painting, likewise, it is imperative to use supreme-quality fragrance oils to make your product last longer. Precise measurement of fragrance oils adds to longevity and better strength. Using a minimal load of fragrance oil will deliver the poor hot and cold throw. To strengthen the scent of your candle, it is important to check the wax type and quality of your fragrance oil. Different waxes offer different hot throws. If fragrance is your only concern, paraffin wax comes out on the top, as this wax is eminent for the best hot throw.

How to fix fragrance fading?

- Use best–formulated fragrance oils made from high-grade material. Low-quality fragrance oils are very volatile, and therefore, the fragrance diminishes quickly. However, the thing to notice here is that a high concentration of fragrance oil will not always lead to better fragrance but rather introduce sweating. You need to stick your load according to the wax recommendations provided by your supplier.

- Use optimal container size and designs. If your container is too wide and has a larger surface area, your fragrance will escape easily. On the flip side, if your design is conservative with narrow or tight openings, it does not allow air ventilation and leads to worse issues.

- Avoid exposing your candles to direct heat or sunlight as it degrades the quality of the wax. If you do not want your fragrance to evaporate, store it in a cool and dark space.

Wax Discoloration

Due to exposure to air and light, the wax encounters yellowish, brownish, and blue stains at the top surface and this is referred to as wax discoloration. This issue is related to the aesthetic and not to the performance of the candle.

Comprehensive Solutions to Candle Issues

What causes Wax discoloration?

When your wax is exposed to air or light, the elements in the wax undergo chemical reactions to form colored compounds. Since the wax and fragrance oils have different compositions, they do not blend well oftentimes, giving rise to intense stains and discoloration. Other possible causes of wax discoloration are the use of dyes, additives, impurities, and temperature fluctuations.

How to fix Wax Discoloration?

- The use of UV-resistant materials, particularly fragrance oil additives and dyes, can avoid discoloration. There should be minimal exposure to light and air.

- Opt for chemicals and fragrance oils that can merge well with wax and not react poorly.

- Use airtight packing while shipping in extreme temperatures, as thermal degradation can cause discoloration.

- If the discoloration has occurred already, melt some wax and add a thin layer to the top.

Wax Cracking

Wax cracking refers to the condition when there are fissures or fractures at the surface of the wax going deep down to the bottom. These waxes vary in depth and size, and it deteriorates the physical appearance as well as the performance of the candle.

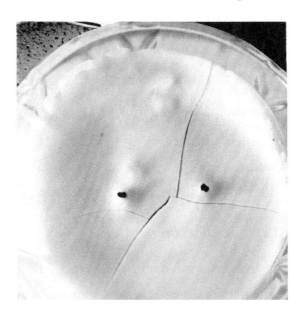

What causes wax cracking?

Wax cracking is typically caused by rapid shifts in temperatures. This means rapid cooling or rapid heating can introduce cracks in the candle. Overheating the wax or heating it in the wrong way can also weaken or alter the properties of wax, which can introduce cracks.

How to fix wax cracking?

- Preheating your containers is highly recommended as it protects the candle from frosting, cracking, and many other issues. This allows the wax to cool at a gradual and constant rate.

- Always opt for the double boiler method and avoid using the oven or other heat sources.

- Avoid using high percentage or dense fragrance oils. Choose light and well-formulated fragrance oils with the best hot and cold throw.

- Adhere to recommended fragrance load guidelines provided by fragrance oil suppliers. Avoid exceeding the maximum recommended fragrance concentration to prevent adverse effects on the wax.

Wax Sweating

Wax sweating is also known as wax bloom, and it refers to the formation of white, cloudy, wet spots at the surface of candles. During the cooling process, the fragrance oils migrate and cause the candles to look ugly.

What causes sweating?

Certain fragrance oils have compounds that do not merge properly and separate themselves from wax. This results in sweat spots. Some waxes with a high percentage of additives may cause sweating.

How to fix Sweating?

High-quality, well-formulated fragrance oils should be added to the wax, followed by constant stirring for up to two minutes. Make sure to heat your wax at around 175-185 F so that your wax and oils bind well with each other. If not heated and stirred properly, the wax will not bind properly with the oil.

- Choose natural waxes that are free from additives.
- Avoid overheating and pour at optimal temperature.
- Store in a dark and cool space.

Chapter 5

Basic Candle Burn Test

The burn test is conducted under controlled conditions for a few hours to measure the performance of candles. The primary goal of performing a burn test is to evaluate whether the wick performs well, the fragrance dissipates properly, and the candle satisfies the aesthetics while adhering to the safety standards. The burn test holds the utmost importance to ensure that your candle does not produce excessive soot, has an unstable flame, and has an appropriate melt pool. For each test, your candle should not exceed the limit of four hours. If you are planning to sell your candles, the burn test contributes to customers' satisfaction and credibility that your candles are safe to use. Following the completion of this test, one becomes sure of using appropriate wick sizes or quality of fragrances. For instance, fragrance and essential oils having thicker viscosity will need a thicker wick to perform safely.

Burn Test Checklist

Before conducting a burn test, make sure that you have the following things prepared.

A candle cured for an appropriate period: It is important that your primary wax has set properly before the burn test. A lack of impatient candle makers conducts burn tests without curing, and this leads to disappointment as not only is the fragrance but also the wick performance compromised. There is no exaggeration that the wax performs differently after it has hardened properly. Use this guide to see how much you need to cure your candles:

- Vegetable wax: 14 days

- Paraffin wax: 2-3 days

- Soy wax- 7-14 days

- Blends: 1 day – 14 days

- A Ruler

- A Scissor

- A Smartphone/ camera to capture photos

- Burn Test Notecards

- A lighter/matchsticks

- A stopwatch

- A pen and a paper

Burn Test Procedure

Organize your test space and place your candle on a leveled heat-resistant surface. It is recommended to use a large tray that is capable of holding the entire liquified wax in case your candle is crafted in glass material that might potentially crack. Make sure to maintain a safe space of at least six inches if you are testing two or more candles. The ideal room temperature for your candle should be around 20 to 30 °C.

It is crucial to preserve a consistent space for each test. This means that if you are testing one candle in a medium-sized room with no drafty conditions, your other candles should share the uniform setup.

Basic Candle Burn Test

Diligently label each candle by highlighting key details about wick size, wax, and fragrance load. In the absence of notecards, you can use sticky notes or else a piece of paper and stick it with tape.

Measure your wick using a ruler and trim the wick to ¼ " or ⅛ " with the help of a wick trimmer. You can also use a nail cutter or a sharp scissor.

Now, grab your lighter and burn your candle. Set your stopwatch to one hour and observe the change in the melt pool. At this point, do not leave your candle unattended.

After each hour, do not forget to capture clear photos of your melt pool and wick condition. Make detailed notes of your melt pool, flame height, sooting, hot throw, and other relevant information.

Following this test, check if your melt pool is adequate for the diameter of your vessel. Ideally, your candles should not have a melt pool more than 1/4 inch from the edges of your container. If it has not attained a full melt pool, this means your wick is too small. In this case, you need to wick up. For instance, if you were previously using a wick of 0.25 thickness, switch to 0.5 thickness.

If your melt pool is deeper than ½ inch, the flame is too high, the vessel is too hot, or there is sooting, this is a sign for you to wick down.

After extinguishing it, let the candle cool and repeat the same procedure again and again until 6 mm of wax remains. Each burn will deliver varied outcomes as the wick will soak up the wax so your melt pool will be slower in the first few burns and accelerate as you repeat the process.

Throughout the entire test procedure, you may encounter tunneling, mushrooming, cracking, etc. Jot down all these candle-related concerns.

ASTM Standards for Burn Test

- According to the ASTM standard for burn tests, your candle should have

- The maximum top flame height less than 3 inches

- Container should not be cracked, broken, or wax spilled from anywhere

- No excessive black smoke or sooting

- The outer temperature of the container should be below 140 °F (60 °C)

Your wick is too large for the container if

- The temperature of your container exceeds 140 F

- The wick is producing excessive black smoke

- The flame height is greater than 3 inches

- The melt pool is too large

Your wick is too small for the container if

- Candle has tunnelled

- The candle has dipped into the wax, and the flame has extinguished

- Wax remains on the edges but burns from the centre

Chapter 6

Decorate and Customize Your Candles

Molds Candles

The decorative candles are in high demand owing to their unique and intricate designs. The makers beautifully craft candles fashioned in diverse shapes and sizes. Typically, the best-selling candle includes products exclusively tailored for religious festivals, birthdays, and weddings. To make the most out of these beautiful designs, it is crucial to understand what techniques we need to employ to end up with top-notch results.

1. **Dried Flower Pillar Candle**

    Dried or pressed flower candles look aesthetically pleasing and offer a soothing ambiance. This modern decorative style embraces timeless beauty and adds a touch of botanical delight. To craft pressed flower pillar candles,

    Gather some random flowers from the garden. The brighter shades of flowers offer a more versatile look than pale ones.

    Arrange all these flowers on absorbent paper.

    Iron the paper. At this point, your steam should be at the very lowest possible temperature.

    Do not move the iron in back-and-forth direction, as it will tear off the delicate flowers.

After your flowers have turned dry and crispy, turn off the steam.

Now, wrap the paper tightly on the candle. Use a heat gun so the flowers can melt and stick to the candle.

After the candle has dried, remove the wax paper slowly, and your decorative pressed flower candle will be ready to use.

2. **Hand painted candles**

Hand-painted candles are one of the adorable ensembles to elevate your home. These candles reflect diverse forms of art with their minimal to vibrant designs and colors. The personalized touch of the handmade element makes them unique and customizable for everyone. For art lovers who want to surround themselves with creativity, hand-painted candles can be a great experiment.

To make hand-painted candles:

The preliminary step is to clean the mold.

Heat the candle, add color and fragrance oil, pour the wax, and de-mold it.

Now, rub the candle with alcohol to create an absorbent surface.

There are a plethora of paints in the market but acrylic paints work best than the rest.

Create different patterns and designs using either a straight or a curved brush.

If you want to paint it without patterns, coat it once, let it dry, and coat it again.

After drying, enjoy your customized painted candle.

Container Candles

If you want your candle to burn for longer and serve the dual function of ambiance and style, container candles are better options. Also, these candles are more aesthetically pleasing, particularly with white colour. However, there are many ways to customize container candles with a diverse range of monochrome and multi-colors, dried flowers, gold foils, and more. The minimal decor of these candles makes them convenient to use for home decor, offices, and several festivals.

1. **Dried flower candles**

   The dried flowers in containers elevate the aesthetics of candles like none other. These mini flowers offer a versatile and modern look with their minimal design. To craft this effortless candle, all you need to do is

   Pour your colored and fragrant wax into mini Molds and de-mold them.

   After your container wax has properly solidified, use a heat gun to level the surface.

   Let it cool for another 10-15 minutes.

   Use a heat gun again, but this time, your temperature settings should be very low.

When your wax is slightly melted, add dried and pressed flowers at specific locations of your choice. It is best to decorate the edges so they do not melt earlier.

Trim your wick and enjoy.

2. **Coloured candles**

   While white candles look aesthetically pleasing, modern and artistic personalities are attracted by colored candles. In this, you can experiment with mono colors, multi colors, layered candles, marbled candles, and more. The room for experimenting with colorful candles is huge.

   For monochrome candles

   The monochrome candles offer a basic yet very empowering effect to use in any setting. Many customers prefer white only as it symbolizes peace, comfort, and elegance. To make monochrome candles:

   Heat the wax using the double boiler method.

   Use candle colors, either liquid gel colors or dyed chips.

   Add fragrance, stir it for two minutes, and then pour it into the container.

   For multi-coloured candles

   Multi-colored candles allow you to have a lot of vibrant or pastel colors in one container. The seamless blend of different colors looks fascinating and adds to the depth of beautiful visuals. To make multi-colour layered candles:

Heat a small quantity of wax, use candle colors, and add fragrance oils.

Pour the wax

Repeat the same process with different colors.

For marble candles

The marbled candles are popular for their complex designs and patterns, which depict a unique piece of art. To make marble candles:

Add a very small quantity of dyed wax at the bottom of the container.

Rotate the container slowly so that the dyed wax is irregularly wrapped around the edges.

Let this thin layer solidify at room temperature, and then add the remaining wax to the container.

Gold foiled candles

The gold color in gold foiled candles embraces luxurious design with its alluring shimmery looks. The white wax when combines with these foils' crafts the most minimal, decent, and sophisticated design to be used on all occasions. To make gold-foiled candles

Stick the foils at the edges of the container using Mod Podge.

Now, add the melted wax to the container.

In the first method, make sure to leave some space for an extra layer. After solidifying, sprinkle some gold foil and add a very thin layer of wax again. This gives an embedded look.

In the second method, pour the wax into the container and let it solidify. After it has solidified, use a heat gun to melt the top layer and add gold foils to stick them properly while ensuring that the foils are visible.

Chapter 7

Best Scent Combinations for Candles

Custom fragrances hold great worth as they cannot be found anywhere. However, finding the best scent combination is the most difficult task since the term *"the best"* is very subjective, depending on people's liking, preferences, seasons, and festivals. While there is a diverse range of fragrances to experiment with, creating well-formulated top scent combinations that match your ambiance and surroundings is challenging. This chapter introduces you to some of the best-selling and sought-after scent combinations.

The initial step is to choose the type of scent you need to work with. This includes floral, woody, spicy, citrus, and many others. The next step is to combine it with a fragrance that strengthens it rather than diminishing it. Combining two harsh and strong scents or two mild scents can be unpleasant. The art of mastering the recipe of scent combination demands an understanding of notes, patience, and testing. Here is an easy guide to major scents that can blend well with other scents.

Scents	Combinations
Floral	Citrus, Spicy, Woody
Woody	Citrus, Spicy, Floral, and Woody
Citrus	Floral, Woody, Citrus, Herbal
Spicy	Floral, Woody, Citrus

Here is another guide for scent combinations in different seasons

Seasons	Surrounding	Combinations
Summer	Floral and Citrus	Rose, Gardenia, Apple, and Orange
Spring	Floral and Fruity	Lemon, Grapefruit, Violet, Jasmine, Rose, Lily, and Iris
Autumn	Earthy and Spicy	Apple, Cinnamon, Vanilla, Musk
Winter	Woody and Earthy	Coffee, Vanilla, Musk

This table introduces you to the scent combinations for different moods

Moods	Combinations
Memorable	Oud
Forest and Earthy	Cedarwood, Cypress tree, and Sandalwood
Bakery	Almond, coconut, vanilla
Relaxation	Lavender with a hint of lemon
Romantic	Rose
Spicy	Apple, Cinnamon, Vanilla, Orange, Clove

The Guide for Notes

There are three notes that we observe in a fragrance: top notes, middle notes, and base notes.

When you lit a candle, the top notes are the notes you smell first. This is the preliminary impression that you get at the very early stage within a few minutes of burning. The top notes are milder and highly volatile in nature, so soft floral or citrus notes that last for a short period of time are normally chosen.

The middle notes are a middle ground of top and base notes and are the most prominent out of the three. These notes stay for a longer period, so strong aromas such as bright florals and spicy notes are commonly used.

Eventually, the base notes add depth and longevity to the fragrance when the candle is extinguished. These notes serve as the last impression, and typically, vanilla, musk, and woody notes are preferred.

The guide for blending

For blending the fragrances to create your own unique and customized aroma, all you need is:

Fragrance oils

Blotting paper

1. Select the type of fragrance you are already familiar with.

2. Dip the blotter paper in the fragrance oil. The red line is a guide of ratio for the first and second fragrances. If you want equal ratios of both, dip to the first line.

3. Let it dry for 1 minute.

4. Smell the fragrance and keep testing.

Best Fragrance Combinations - Year Round

Lavender

Lavender and Vanilla: The strong scent of lavender, when combined with the sweet and mild smell of vanilla, offers an enriching fragrance. This is a perfect balance between floral and sweet notes that have healing properties such as better sleep or reduced anxiety.

Lavender and Lemon: The floral and citrus notes complement each other well. The fragrance starts with lemon, which might be a little unpleasing but settles with lavender, providing a serene experience.

Vanilla

Apple cherry and vanilla: All these three fragrances are very common and give more bakery or apple pie vibes. This scent is ideal for people preferring natural sweet notes embracing sweet memories and positive vibes.

Vanilla with coffee and caramel: Vanilla with coffee and caramel is one of the underrated but best scent combinations. A larger part of the fragrance is covered by coffee with a quarter of vanilla and a bit of caramel that blend together to offer a rich, luxurious cafe setting.

Plum

Plum and Cardamom: The plum and cardamom combine floral and spicy notes that eventually burst with a luxurious scent combination. Cardamom has a very fresh scent that blends well with woody and spicy notes.

Eucalyptus

Eucalyptus and Lavender: Eucalyptus has an aromatic and fresh scent that is often associated with healing and rejuvenation. When this aromatic scent combines with floral notes such as lavender, it gives off a harmonious balance of super refreshing and floral fragrance.

Eucalyptus and Mint: The Eucalyptus Mint combination is a super refreshing blend with a cool and mentholated aroma. For people dealing with anxiety or sleep disorders, this is a perfect cool and crisp combination offering spa-like vibes at home.

Sandalwood

Sandalwood and Musk: Sandalwood has a warm woody fragrance, while musk has sweet and woody notes, which are normally used in base notes. Sandalwood is known for its soothing properties, and when it combines with musk, it blends well to give off a beautiful earthy and woody fragrance. In this combination, sandalwood will prevail with a hint of musk to offer depth and complexity.

Sandalwood and Rose: Rose has a strong and rich floral fragrance and is often associated with evoking romantic vibes. The warm notes of sandalwood complement the rich floral notes of rose to offer a luxurious scent.

Sandalwood and Patchouli: Patchouli has an earthy and musky fragrance with some spicy undertones. This fragrance is often used for meditations to create balance in life. When combined with sandalwood, the exotic and mysterious scent.

Chapter 8

Starting A Homemade Candle Business

If candle making is your favourite hobby, you might have thought of starting your own candle business and being called *"an entrepreneur"* at some point. Starting a candle business provides you an opportunity to showcase your creative skills in the growing market of home decor. This chapter will serve as a framework to launch your own scented candles business from scratch. From production to marketing, this guide will explore intricate but valuable insights to stand out from others.

Should you start a candle business?

Candles have gained popularity in the last few years and now serve as an essential home decor. Beyond their conventional purpose of lighting, these candles are a symbol of relaxation and a soothing experience. According to the research, the global interest in homemade candles is increasing exponentially, and the candle industry will reach 64 billion by 2027. Nowadays, this product is not only set as a centerpiece in homes but used in restaurants, salons, and offices to enhance the mood. Here are multiple reasons to start a candle business

1. Cost may vary. You can either use cheap materials or expensive materials.

2. Easy to sell from physical stores to online platforms.

3. Easy customisation

4. Can launch a huge line of your collection

5. Earn a good profit from your home

Step by Step guide to Starting your Candle Business

Jot Down Your Budget

Once you have mastered the art of making long-lasting scented candles with testing, it's time to put your efforts into use by selling them. First, you need to make a business plan that includes your budget, candlemaking essentials, delivery charges, and all your expenses. All these things demand strategic plans and financial management that can serve as a roadmap through different stages of production and operation. Allocating a budget helps you to have a clear vision of your expenses and foresee future challenges. This is how you are going to allot your budget.

Material	Wax, Fragrances, Wick, Container, Dyes, Tools
Packaging essentials	Shipping boxes, labels, Bags, Business Cards
Marketing	Website, Social Media Advertising
Operational Cost	Workspace rent (if any), Legal Compliance

Conduct Market Research

Thorough market research is imperative for any business, which incorporates gathering and analysing information on market prices, target audience, and competitors. Before launching your products at a great scale, understanding your target audience becomes necessary to comprehend their trends, preferences, and any gaps that you can fill through your creativity.

To conduct market research, visit websites that sell candle making products and e-commerce stores such as Amazon or Ali Express and write down the price of the material, shipping cost, delivery time, reviews, and other relevant details. These details are then compared with the local vendors or wholesalers.

Plan Your Product Line

Before launching your product line, you need to put yourself into the customer's shoes and ask a few critical questions, like:

- Will this product be beneficial for them?

- If you were the customer, would you have bought it?

- Is the price reasonable, and will the customers be willing to pay it?

This helps you to add value to your products and surpass customers' expectations. Once you have got your answers, write down your products with quantity. For instance,

- White Soy Container candle= 10

- Fragrances (Coffee, Lavender, Vanilla, Eucalyptus, Orange/ 2 each)

- Flower Mold candles= 3

- Fragrances= Iris, Jasmine, Rose

- Colours= White, Pink, Red

The diverse range of designs and fragrances will target different season-based occasions and personal preferences. By carefully launching your product line, you can offer a compelling range that can excite and persuade the audience and eventually drive more sales.

Create Brand

After allocating budget and planning your product line, it's time to name your brand. Your brand name should not solely be easy to remember or pronounce but deliver a compelling story that sets you apart from your competitors. The act of storytelling not only engages the audience but drives more sales. A good brand ensures loyalty and transparency, particularly in a challenging and highly saturated industry. Whereas the art of storytelling is the foundation to grow, communicate, and resonate

Here are some of the examples of brand names:

- The Candle Cottage: Symbolise home and warm feelings.
- Craft her candles: Symbolise creativity and attention to detail.
- Wick and Wonders: Offers magical properties of candles through their best fragrances.
- Flickering Aroma: Depicts light, which symbolizes relaxation.

Create Brand Logo

A lot of candle makers use AI or free tools to make logos. While these may sound convenient since your brand story should be reflected by your logo, it should be customized. Your logo should be minimal and not too extra with colors like whites and pastels. This is because it's a home-decor business that should offer vibes of comfort and coziness.

While there are too many apps and websites to create your custom logos, Adobe being the finest of all, we recommend using *Canva* as it is beginner friendly. This website has tons of features, and most importantly, it offers millions of free templates that can be customized as per your preference.

Here is a step-by-step guide to using Canva

1. Visit Canva at canva.com
2. Click the blue "create a design" option at the top right side of the screen.
3. Write "logo" and select the appropriate dimensions.
4. In the design section, select your favorite template
5. Use your desired elements, fonts, font size, and pictures to customize your logo.
6. Click the "share" option at the top right side of the screen and download your logo in the desired format.

Visual Appearance

After successfully crafting your logo, you need to show your strong online presence on diverse platforms. The easiest way is to set up an Instagram page, mentioning details of the name and bio and inserting the logo. You can make a separate page for Facebook and TikTok so that it reaches a larger target audience. Etsy is an incredible platform for selling homemade products to people who admire artistic work. According to the research, Facebook has more than 2.8 billion users, Instagram has 1 billion active members, and TikTok has 1.2 billion active members, which makes them ideal platforms for engagement. All these platforms seamlessly work together to showcase your business, connect with your target audience, and drive sales.

Customise Labels

Customized labels are pre-eminent in the candle business. With the right information and attention to detail, you can make custom labels that catch the attention of the customers. To make customized labels, all you need to do is to decide the dimensions of your container. Once decided, prepare each label of diverse fragrances via *Canva.* There are templates to choose from, but most importantly, the list should incorporate the fragrance name, wax type, burn time, and amount of wax used. The other details are not as mandatory as the four factors listed above. While designing, it is critical to keep the design simple with white and pastel colors for clarity. Your customized labels set you apart from your competitors by adding a touch of professionalism and value to your brand identity. Once the labels are customized, you can use *Avery* to make a sheet of labels and print them out together to save your label cost in the long run.

Price Your Product Line

Remember, your cost may vary more than others because of differences in demographics. A seller selling in the US cannot compare their rates with a seller selling candles in the UK. It is an unrealistic approach. Profit, too, is a subjective thing. Some sellers offer super reasonable products, but with good marketing, they eventually make a good profit with a high number of orders. On the contrary, others make huge profits with minimal orders. To know your profit, mention the price of each material with quantity and sum them. This is how you are going to make calculations:

1 Container= $4.5

150 g Soy Wax= $3

Wick= $0.3

Fragrance oil 13 ml= $1.7

Dye= $0.5

Additional cost (electricity) = $5

If this all sums up to $15, you need to do market research and see if you sell it for $25 (with $10 as your profit). Are people willing to buy it? If yes, it's great; otherwise, you will have to reduce your cost by buying a bit cheaper quality material or maybe buying from other sources that cost you less.

Introduce it to Your Friends and Family

Launching a small business is an exciting and huge achievement. Before officially launching, you need to introduce your business to your family and close circle. Offering some mini-size samples to your friends will help you get honest feedback on how well your candle performs, particularly with hot and cold throws. These suggestions and feedback provide room for improvement so you can refine your candles and seek areas of growth.

Ways to Stand Out in Your Business

Consistent Visual Presence

Visual presence is not a matter of one day, one week or a month. Only a consistent visual presence can hold a strong impression in the saturated market. Maintain and regularly update social media platforms with fresh content, pictures, reels, and customer testimonials to offer credibility to your customers. Nowadays, fun content gets more views, so strategic planning and making reels on viral music, viral trends, and behind-the-scenes glimpses can get you more visibility with less effort.

The Instagram feature of "scheduling" allows you to create content and post it at a specific time when a greater number of active followers are using it. Audience interaction through polls or QnAs is a fun and simple activity that has maximum impact on your brand growth. Implementing a content calendar helps maintain a steady stream and grow your business in no time.

Monitor analytics by observing audience demographics and engagement matrices. Use that data to make future content. For example, if your one reel gets more viral than others, observe the key features. This includes posting time, photography, type of music, or even hashtags. Mastering the art of social media algorithms is the gateway to reaching a target audience. Some social media platforms, such as Facebook and Instagram, use geotargeting features to display your content in nearby regions, but it cannot be the sole driver. You need to thoroughly understand and comprehend social media algorithms.

Deals and Discounts

Offering deals and discounts can attract new customers with your price promotions. This is a very important strategy to generate buzz around your products. Introducing limited-time promotions, particularly on festivals such as Christmas, Eid, and Holi, can encourage customers to purchase your products. Bundled products in terms of deals not only add value and persuade your customers to shop but earn you a good amount of profit as well. Referral discounts towards future purchases also drive customers and expand your audience. With deals or a high number of purchases, you can offer free delivery or complimentary gifts to engage and enhance the customer experience.

Photography

Visually appealing photography plays a critical role in conveying your brand aesthetic and capturing your audience's attention. If you can't afford to pay highly professional photographers, you can always capture through your phone and edit them with free software such as Lightroom. Lightening techniques coupled with editing skills, angles, arrangements, and props elevate the overall visual appeal of your products and showcase your quality. Your photography should be a mix of closeup shorts with attention to detail through decorative items. You can incorporate flowers, vases, books, and other decorative elements into minimal yet professional shots. Proper optimization for your online platforms, which includes high-resolution images, correct size, and proper file format, ensures good display on social media.

On-site presence

Expanding your business beyond your online presence can boost your visibility and offer memorable experiences to your customers. This means setting up an online store or festival stall to stand out in your business. Selecting the right platform for your business is critical. For candle stores, the most popular options are Shopify and Etsy, which offer homemade products with customization options. For festivals, research the local markets and build good relationships with the vendors to have in-depth details of festivals. Design an eye-catching display using lights, signs, and creative props that attract customers. Collecting customer information to stay in touch for future discounts and giveaways to nurture relationships in the longer run.

Glossary

Cold throw: The intensity of scent that dissipates in your surroundings when the candle is not lit. A strong cold throw indicates a good-quality candle.

Hot throw: The intensity of scent that dissipates in your surroundings when the candle is burning. A strong hot throw indicates a good-quality candle.

Flashpoint: The temperature at which the wax has vaporized enough to ignite in the open flame. Flashpoint is crucial for the safety consideration of the candle.

Cure time: The period of time up to which the candle should not be burnt to reach its peak performance of hot and cold throw. A fully cured candle offers the best performance.

Wax pool: The amount of melted wax that has reached the edges of the container. A full-melt pool ensures even burning and maximized fragrance release.

Fragrance Load: The optimal percentage of fragrance oil that should be added for a strong fragrance release.

Melt point: The temperature at which a candle starts to melt.

Burn time: The total period of time when the candle has burnt.

Additives: The substances that are added to the candle to enhance the performance.

Frost point: The temperature at which wax begins to harden and form white frost-like crystalline patterns on the surface of the candle.

Wax blend: A mixture of different types of waxes catered to your requirements.

Wick performance: The performance of the wick in terms of fragrance release, burn pool, soot, flame size, and burn rate in the candle.

🎇 **Join Our Crafting Community!** 🎇

Hello Creative Soul,

If you've found joy and inspiration in the pages of our book, we've got something special for you. Become a part of our exclusive mailing list! It's more than just an email subscription; it's your gateway to a world of crafting wonders. Here's what you'll get:

📙 Exclusive Sneak Peeks: Be the first to see what's coming. Get early glimpses of our upcoming books that continue to explore the art of crafting.

🎨 Personalized Content: Tailored tips, tricks, and tutorials that resonate with your crafting journey. Enhance your skills with content you can't find anywhere else.

📚 Member-Only Offers: Enjoy special discounts, offers, and opportunities exclusive to our subscribers.

📝 Direct Line to the Author: Share your thoughts, feedback, and what you'd like to see next.

Your input directly influences our future creations!

Joining is easy! Simply:

Visit the Link: https://bit.ly/3PnRASC

OR, Use the QR Code:

*We value your privacy and creativity.
Your email will be used solely to enhance your crafting journey with us.

Made in the USA
Middletown, DE
05 May 2025

75167850R00066